To a Stradivarius Violin

O precious treasury of sounds exquisite,
The music of all time within thee sings!
Old melodies, and quaint strange whisperings
Of bye-gone songs that linger and invite.
Earth's cry of pain, heaven's anthems of delight,
The hopes and fears of love's imaginings,
All found a voice upon thy thrilling strings!
Thou singest still, with changes infinite,
The heights and depths of this strange human life
With all its sorrows and its ecstasies,
Its thoughts unuttered, its most voiceless cries;
One pure tone rising always through the strife
Intense, heart-searching. Sorrow in such setting
Is a sweet dream and a more sweet forgetting.

F. S. (*thought to be Federico Sacchi*)

From "The Salabue Stradivari." A History of the Famous Violin Known as "Le Messie." E. W. Hill and Sons, London

THE STRADIVARI MEMORIAL

Stradivari

That plain, white-aproned man who stood at work
Patient and accurate, full fourscore years;
Cherished his sight and touch by temperance;
And, since keen sense is love of perfectness,
Made perfect Violins, the needed paths
For inspiration and high mastery.

George Eliot

The instrument on which he played
Was in Cremona's workshops made
By a great master of the past
Ere yet was lost the art divine.
Fashioned of maple and of pine
That in Tyrolean forests vast
Had rocked and wrestled with the blast;
Exquisite was it in design,
A marvel of the lutist's art,
Perfect in each minutest part.
And in its hollow chamber, thus,
The maker from whose hands it came
Had written his unrivaled name —
" Antonius Stradivarius."

Longfellow

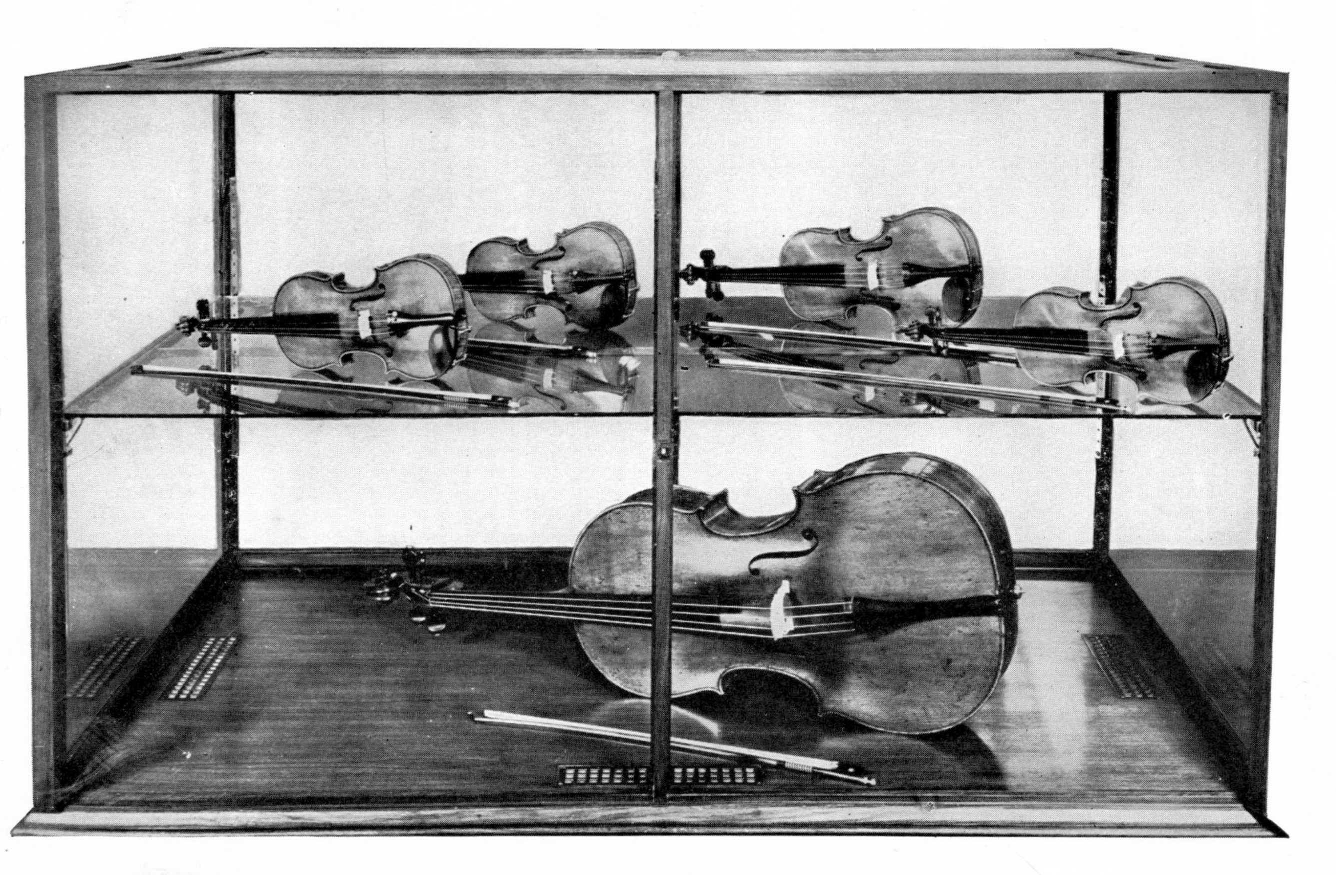

THE STRADIVARI INSTRUMENTS IN THEIR CASE

The Stradivari Memorial

AT

WASHINGTON, THE NATIONAL CAPITAL

BY

WILLIAM DANA ORCUTT

Library of Congress

GERTRUDE CLARKE WHITTALL FOUNDATION

DESIGNED BY WILLIAM DANA ORCUTT
AND PRINTED AT THE PLIMPTON PRESS
UNDER HIS PERSONAL SUPERVISION

Foreword

Any work of art that endures is a real message to the world from an artist who feels impelled to release it from his soul through the medium in which he works. These messages are expressed in different *media* — in stone, on canvas, or in type. Antonio Stradivari found that he could best express his message through an instrument so exquisitely devised and executed that each note drawn from the strings by an artist reached the world in richer beauty because of that coöperation.

The impulse which initiates these messages, regardless of the method, is the same. Cobden-Sanderson, the great English bookbinder, once said: "When I bind and decorate a volume, I seem to be setting myself, like a magnetized needle, or like an ancient temple, in line and all square, not alone with my own ideal of society, but with that orderly and rhythmical whole which is the revelation of science and the normal of developed humanity." This is what Michelangelo did when he produced his great sculptures, Raphael his superb paintings, Shakespeare his immortal writings, and Stradivari his magnificent instruments.

After the great artist has produced his message-bearing masterpiece, he is at the mercy of the world. In literature the risk of loss is minimized because the great writer's productions are multiplied through the printing press; but in Art these messages are unique, and as such can never be replaced. Fortunately for the artist, wealth often prompts and encourages the collector's instinct; fortunately for the world, that first desire for acquisition and possession on the part of wealthy patrons of the Arts grows into the greater desire to make these masterpieces available to the masses to whom they would otherwise be denied.

We are familiar, particularly in America, with this instinct to perpetuate and to share, as expressed in the great Art collections assembled and made accessible to the public. The recent establishment of the Stradivari Memorial, in the Library of Congress at Washington, the National Capital, is the sole instance on record, so far as known, where absolute permanence has been guaranteed to the great Master's work. Stradivari made in all, it is said, over eleven hundred instruments, but there are only about six hundred extant today. These are scattered over the world, mostly in the prized possession of private owners. Five noble examples of his genius are now placed for all time to come in a permanent home, assured — insofar as is humanly possible to foresee — security and proper physical care, to be seen and admired in our Nation's treasure house. Moreover, through the far-reaching foresight and generosity of their collector and donor, they are consecrated in perpetuity to vital public service on the concert stage by distinguished artists.

Every great work of art gathers about itself history and associations as it passes from the hands of its creator and survives the centuries. This is particularly true of these Stradivari instruments. The genesis of the idea which brought the Collection into being; the drama underlying the acquisition of the various instruments; the details surrounding their acceptance by the United States Government; the fundamental motives and purposes connected with the Memorial itself — all combine into a human story worth perpetuating. To the telling of that brief story this volume is dedicated.

The Magic of the Strad

THAT MYSTERY SHOULD SHROUD THE PERSONAL HISTORY of a man who died only two centuries ago, who produced masterpieces in his art during seventy years of actual labor, and who attained fame before his death, seems incredible — yet the fact remains that even the slight data concerning the life of Antonio Stradivari, master violin-maker of Cremona and of the world, is based upon such fugitive foundations as to be contradictory and almost unreliable. The bi-centenary of his death, celebrated in Cremona in the Spring of 1937, added to the historic records of Stradivari's famous instruments, but not an iota to the insufficient knowledge of their maker's personality or personal history. Yet, after all, what more glorious or enduring biography could a genius seek than to have his name and memory kept alive forever through the living expression of his creations!

There seems to be some doubt even that Stradivari was born in Cremona, and the date of his birth, 1644, is arrived at only through the label of one of his instruments. The pride taken by the master-maker in the amazing vitality he possessed in his old age prompted him to record his years in his own handwriting on the label of his last violin, *Antonius Stradivarius Cremonensis Faciebat Annus 1737, d'Anni 93*. His death, however, is officially recorded as of December 18, 1737, on the books of the Church of S. Matteo. That his father was Alessandro Stradivari, a cloth merchant, is also fully established. His education was obviously slight, as the few existing letters written by him are scarcely literate.

Antonio was married twice, and the issue of both marriages was eleven children, of whom only three enter into his later history. Francesco and Omobono, his elder sons, continued their father's business at the same location, but failed to add lustre to the Stradivari name. On Omobono's death, Francesco continued by himself, and when he died he left all the family property to his younger brother, Paolo, a cloth merchant. Of Paolo we learn most from a series of letters between him and the Count Cozio de Salabue, who purchased these relics. Francesco had originally inherited ninety-one violins, two violoncellos, and several violas, in addition to the inlaid set of instruments his father had made to present to Philip V of Spain. Most of these instruments had been sold by Francesco or Paolo before Count Salabue took possession of the tools and assets, but the famous "Messie," made by Antonio in 1716, and cherished by him throughout his life, was included in the purchase.

Some authorities state that Antonio was buried in the family crypt in the Chapel of the Rosary in the Church of San Domenico in Cremona, but when this church was torn down in 1869 no care was taken to identify or preserve the relics of those interred there.

All that we know regarding the personal appearance of Stradivari is found in a biography published by François Joseph Fétis in 1856:

"The life of Anthony Stradiuarius was as tranquil as his calling was peaceful. The year 1702, alone, must have caused him much disquiet, when, during the war concerning the succession, the city of Cremona was taken by Marshal Villeroy on the Imperialist side, retaken by Prince Eugène, and finally taken a third time by the French; but after that period Italy enjoyed a long tranquillity, in which the old age of the artist glided peacefully away. We know but little respecting that uneventful existence. Polledro, late first Violin at the Chapel Royal of Turin, who died a few years ago at a very advanced age, declared that his master had known Stradiuarius, and that he was fond of talking about him. He was, he said, tall and thin, habitually covered with a cap of white wool, and of cotton in Summer. He wore over his clothes an apron of white leather when he worked, and, as he was always working, his costume scarcely ever varied. He had acquired more than competency by labour and economy, for the inhabitants of Cremona were accustomed to say, 'As rich as Stradiuarius!' "

George Hall states (*The Violin*, 1880) that "the house Stradivari occupied stood in the Piazza Roma, formerly called the Square of San Domenico, in the centre of which was the church of the same name."

The statement by Fétis that Stradivari "was always working" is amply borne out by the fact that between the dates of his earliest signed instrument (1666) and his last (1737), the year of his death, he produced 1116 violins, violas, and violoncellos, besides unrecorded viols-da-gamba, pochettes, and guitars. Of these, according to Hill (*Antonio Stradivari*, 1902) 540 violins, 12 violas, and 50 violoncellos are still in existence, in various conditions and completeness—a high tribute to the esteem in which the Stradivari instruments have always been held by the museums, churches, and private individuals who have been their possessors.

The tradition that Stradivari was an apprentice of Nicolò Amati (1598–1684), grandson of the founder of the great Amati house of violin-makers, rests upon a label in an instrument said to be still in existence: "*Antonius Stradiuarius Cremonensis Alumnus Nicolai Amati Faciebat Anno 1666*," and the fact that from 1668 to 1685 his violins resembled the small, delicately constructed models of the older master.

Hart accepts only a part of this statement: " I am not aware," he writes, " that there has ever appeared a violin of Stradiuarius in which it is stated that he was a pupil of Nicholas Amati, or that this assumption has been maintained on any other grounds than the indisputable evidence furnished by the early instruments of this great maker. Never has the affinity in the art of violin-manufacture been more marked than that between Stradiuarius and Nicholas Amati during the early life of the former."

Hill (*Antonio Stradivari*, 1902) states that a violin bearing this label passed through his hands, and he reproduces the label in his volume, thus substantiating the tradition. He continues: " The tone of the violins (Stradivari) made previous to 1684 cannot be distinguished from the average medium-sized Amati. There is the same bright soprano, woody quality of perfect purity, that freedom of response which is so helpful to the average player."

Working as Stradivari did, with no apparent attempt at secrecy during his seventy years of active labor in Cremona, it seems incredible that no accurate notes should have come down through expressions of apprentices (his two sons, Francesco and Omobono, and Carlo Bergonzi), fellow-workers, or neighbors, to throw some light upon his methods, the sources of his material, or the means by which his wealthy patrons learned of his genius.

That Stradivari's reputation was far flung is clearly indicated. In 1682, Michele Monzi commissioned him to make a complete set of instruments for King James II, of England; in 1685, Cardinal Orsini, Bishop of Benevento, ordered a violoncello and two violins to be presented to the Duke of Natalona in Spain; in 1686, the Duke of Medina commissioned Stradivari to make a violoncello for him; in 1702, the Marquis Giovanni Battista Tozalba, General of Cavalry and Governor of Cremona, sent for Stradivari, and after complimenting him for his "peculiar genius," commissioned him to make two violins and a violoncello, which were sent as presents to the Duke of Alba; in 1707 the Marquis Desiderio Clari "wrote by order of King Charles III of Spain commissioning Stradivarius to make six violins, two tenors, and one 'cello for the Royal orchestra"; and, in 1715, the Elector of Poland ordered twelve violins.

Returning to Hart's incredulity regarding the 1666 violin of Stradivari containing the statement that he was a pupil of Amati: Hart accepts the similarity between the early instruments of Stradivari and those of Amati as being a sufficiently sound argument upon which to base the statement of the apprenticeship. "We have seen instruments bearing the signature of Nicholas Amati," Hart writes, "which can be readily recognized by a practiced judge as being the work of Stradiuarius, in some cases *in toto* . . . in other cases, and more frequently, in part, as when the beautiful scroll of Stradiuarius is met with on the body of an Amati, or the sound hole of such an instrument shows that it has been cut by the hand of Stradiuarius. We will not, however, consider these instruments as typical of the maker, but pass on to the period when we assume that Stradiuarius left the workshop of Amati, in the year 1668. At this point we find that his whole work is in accordance with the plans of Amati (not as seen in the latter's *grand pattern*, but in his ordinary full-sized instrument); the arching is identical, the corners are treated similarly, the sound hole is quite Amati-like in form, yet easily distinguished by its extreme delicacy; the scroll a thorough imitation of Amati, and presenting a singular contrast to the vigorous individuality which Stradiuarius displayed in this portion of his work a few years later." To this statement Hill takes exception.

During Stradivari's second period, dating from 1686 to 1694, his instruments are marked by a distinct difference from those of Amati in every particular. Again quoting from Hart: "The sound hole, which is a masterpiece of gracefulness, reclines more. The curves of the middle bouts are more extended than in this maker's later instruments. The corners are brought out, although not prominently so. Here, too, we notice the change in the formation of the scroll. He suddenly leaves the form that he had hitherto imitated, and follows the dictates of his own fancy. The result is bold and striking, and even leaves the impression on the mind that it partakes much of the character belonging to the bodies of instruments of his latter period. . . . The varnish on the instruments belonging to the period under consideration is varied. Sometimes it is a rich golden colour, deliciously soft and transparent; in other instances Stradiuarius has used varnish of a deeper hue, which might be described as light red, the quality of which is also very beautiful. We find this varnish chiefly on those instruments where he has made his back in two parts. The purfling is narrower than that afterwards used."

There has been much discussion regarding the effect of Stradivari's varnishes upon the tone of his instruments: "The idea that the varnish of a violin has some influence upon its tone," Hart writes, "has often been ridiculed. . . . That the varnish does influence the tone there is strong proof. The finest varnishes are those of oil, and they require the utmost skill and patience in their use. They dry very slowly, and may be described as of a soft and yielding nature. . . . A violin varnished with fine oil-varnish takes time to mature, and will not bear forcing in any way. At first the instrument is somewhat muffled, as the pores of the wood have become impregnated with oil. This makes the instrument heavy both in weight and sound; but, as time rolls on, the oil dries, leaving the wood mellowed and wrapped in an elastic covering which yields to the tone of the instrument, and imparts to it much of its own softness."

The Cremonese varnish, used by Stradivari, Guarneri, and Bergonzi was a composition peculiar to itself, and all efforts to discover the exact formula have been futile. It is supposed that a gum, common at that period, ceased for some reason to be a marketable commodity, and thus passed out of existence.

In selecting his wood, Stradivari generally used maple for the backs, sides, and heads, and a fine quality of pine for the bellies. After 1684 he substituted a finer quality of imported maple, together with poplar and sycamore. The imported stock added to the beauty rather than to the quality of the instruments. Hill comments: "That Stradivari brought to bear a certain amount of judgment in the selection of his materials is beyond discussion, but that he possessed any special knowledge other than that of an intelligent craftsman well versed in the tradition of his craft we are constrained to deny. Take his pre-1684 instruments: all those known to us (with but few exceptions) are made, back, sides, and head, from home-grown maple of a decidedly plain appearance. Acoustically good, it is true, yet not what either he—or we, let us say—would have chosen with choice unfettered. We are therefore forced to conclude either that he was poorly paid for these examples, or that the handsome and sonorous wood he used in later years was then unobtainable. The truth probably lies between these two conclusions: his remuneration was relatively small, and handsome, foreign maple fairly expensive, possibly not to be had at all during certain years."

The year 1700 marks the time when Stradivari stood firmly upon his own feet, having tested out through the two previous periods all that he had found good in the work of his predecessors. He was now fifty-six years old, yet he seemed to exercise his talent with new vigor and originality. He changed the outline of his model, blending the curves one into another as they never had been blended before. Changes are also noted in the treatment of the corners; a wood with a broad curl (much handsomer though not necessarily possessing more beautiful acoustical properties) is used for the backs and sides; the scrolls are more boldly conceived and even more finely executed. The varnish is unusually rich (*See* the "Betts" and "Ward" violins, pages 28 and 32.)

Those violins which the Master made during the seventeen years that remained of his life, while more rugged and lacking in the delicacy of line, in the rounding of the curves, and the appearance of the varnishes, have never been surpassed in tone by instruments of any other period. It was natural that the violins produced toward the end of Stradivari's life should contain evidences of unsteadiness of hand and of physical weakening. Yet no one would question the tone quality of the "Muntz," made in 1736, when Stradivari was ninety-two years old!

All his later instruments were based upon the model of 1700, and vary only in detail. During the years from 1704 to 1720, Hill writes, "we find occasional divergences in pattern, in some cases intentional, no doubt, as it is improbable that all Stradivari's patrons required the greater sonority of tone. Many of the *dilettanti*, the Roman Catholic ecclesiastic, and the elderly aristocrat preferred the dulcet, easy-speaking tone of the smaller Amati, and this must account for the smaller sized 'Strads' which we find occasionally interspersed between the larger types. Sometimes, too, the nature of the wood in the back, though handsome, has caused a lack of sonority. At other times the belly wood is plainly responsible for the want of brilliancy; or occasionally the varnish, or model, is to blame. But with these reservations, what a marvelous result do these sixteen years give us! Instrument after instrument of wonderful tone, the notable points of his predecessors' instruments happily welded into a whole of surpassing merit — sufficient of the noble breadth and sonority of the Maggini combined with the brightness and woodiness of the Amati, and at the same time a flexibility of tone as a whole, thus placing in the hands of the player of average capabilities an instrument as efficient for him as for a great and inspired performer."

During 1720–1722, Stradivari made still another type of violin, differing in tone from anything he had yet produced, — "a type," Hill writes, "although of medium dimensions, presenting, owing to the square appearance of the outline and sound hole, flatness of the arching, etc., an unusually sturdy and robust appearance, though somewhat inelegant. Special features of the tone are a vigorous and incisive power, less flexible and less easy in production, and a quality slightly metallic, suggestive of that of a fine Joseph Guarnerius del Gesù or a Carlo Bergonzi, which undoubtedly this type of violin foreshadows."

The bi-centenary of Stradivari's death, commemorated in Cremona in 1937, renewed the universal interest in the man and his productions, and revived the mythical tradition of "the secret of the Strad." To discover this "secret" has been the quest of hundreds of enthusiasts. It has resulted in confusing even the scant knowledge which can be reliably accepted. Even forgeries have been indulged in to prove pet theories regarding Stradivari's life, methods of working, and materials.

There is but one reason why other violin-makers may not have produced instruments equal in every way to those which bear the Master's signature. Others have employed wood of equal quality, they have successfully imitated the dimensions and the joinery of the various parts. Stradivari's contemporaries at least had access to varnishes made of the same ingredients. What other makers lack is simply that something which cannot be imitated, which cannot be analyzed, which cannot be explained — that gift of consummate genius which delivers its message to the world through the finger-tips of those few children of God anointed among their fellows as chosen for that purpose.

Antonius Stradivarius Cremonensis Facibat Anno 1690

What voices hast thou heard, what hands obeyed,
What love sustained, what lonely vigils blest,
Of those who now are silent and at rest,
Since thy great maker's hand was on thee laid
In far Cremona, and thy fabric made,
Strong, resonant, of beauty manifest,
In delicate amber like a garment drest,
A type of perfect art no time can fade.
What memories haunt thee of that glorious hour
When wakened by a master's hand, thy voice,
First thrilled with passionate, heart compelling power,
Making thy listeners tremble and rejoice;
As the rich tide of music swept along
In highest ecstasy of wordless song!

F. S. (*thought to be Federico Sacchi*)

From "The Tuscan Strad. A Short Account of a Stradivarius Violin." E. W. Hill and Sons, London

The Gertrude Clarke Whittall Foundation

Mrs. Matthew John Whittall is one of those unusual persons who has always looked upon the possession of wealth as something to be accounted for as a trust rather than as being merely a happy incident. The Gertrude Clarke Whittall Foundation, which represents her gift to the American Nation of three violins, a viola, a violoncello — all priceless masterpieces of Stradivari; five matchless bows made by Tourte; and a maintaining fund, is simply the largest and most public of her benefactions, from which she continues to draw human dividends unaffected by depression. The story which leads up to the gathering together of this Collection and its final presentation, which ensures not only the permanent preservation of these instruments, but their continued service to the world as living voices, is scarcely less interesting than that which surrounds the history of the instruments themselves.

Mrs. Whittall frequently attended the world-famous Chamber Music Concerts sponsored by Elizabeth Sprague Coolidge in the beautiful auditorium given by her to the Library of Congress, many years ago. These happy memories prompted Mrs. Whittall to offer her rare Collection to the Library of Congress. She met, for the first time, the Librarian, Herbert Putnam, who entertained the offer with great enthusiasm. Plans matured rapidly. The instruments were placed temporarily in a glass case in the Rare Book Room of the Library. They are now permanently enshrined in the Whittall

Pavilion, adjacent to the Coolidge Auditorium, where they may be seen and admired by all who come to the Library.

The acceptance of this gift secured for these marvelous instruments an enduring home; but that was only a part of Mrs. Whittall's vision. When Paganini died, he bequeathed his famous Guarneri violin to the museum in Genoa, where it has since then been carefully preserved in a glass case. But violins deteriorate unless kept in use, so this instrument, made famous by the great master Paganini, is now practically useless for concert purposes. Mrs. Whittall determined to prevent a repetition of this tragedy. The instruments must not only be preserved, but they must be kept alive to convey to the world through their incomparable tones the beautiful notes imprisoned in them by their master-maker.

Under the terms of the gift these instruments may never be taken from the Library of Congress except for necessary restoration or repair. These conditions prevented their being a part of the celebration of the bi-centenary exercises in Cremona in the Spring of 1937; but the condition is undoubtedly wise. If the instruments were once allowed to be taken abroad or to be withdrawn for concerts in other cities, the risk of injury or destruction would always exist.

To overcome the deprivation which this necessitates to many people who would enjoy hearing these marvelous instruments, plans are being made for an increasing number of concerts open to the public in the Coolidge Auditorium of the Library of Congress; and, furthermore, frequent broadcasts will be made, similar to those already given, to enable the world to listen in. The most distinguished artists, as well as outstanding ensembles will be engaged for performances of chamber music, the expense being provided for by the income from the Gertrude Clarke Whittall Foundation, and the musicians will play upon these Stradivari instruments

GERTRUDE CLARKE WHITTALL

daughter of Henry Tefft and Martha Fielding Clarke
married Matthew John Whittall, of Worcester
Massachusetts, June 4, 1907

From Miniature painted by Laura Hills

instead of upon their own. In addition to these programs, each year on December 18, there will be a special program in commemoration of the anniversary of the death of Stradivari.

Speaking of the different instruments, Mrs. Whittall once said to a friend: " The three violins are as different as human beings. They have strong personality: the ' Betts ' is of royalty; it is outstanding in beauty and perfection, and, as Walt Whitman once said of Mt. Shasta, ' Alone as God.' The ' Castelbarco ' is feminine. The ' Ward ' is sophisticated — it lived long in London and knows so many things. The ' Cassavetti ' is marvelous. A viola, when played by a great artist, can wring your heart. It can express secret thoughts that you have felt and never could put into words. It can say unsayable things. As for the ' Castelbarco ' 'cello, any artist who has once drawn his bow across its strings will be haunted forever by its unforgettable tone. When all the strings are playing together the ensemble is like a heavenly choir, for they all speak the same language."

At the time of Mrs. Whittall's first and only broadcast, Saturday evening, December 18, 1937, she said: " This Collection of instruments I held in trust for a short time. Now they belong to every one of you, for they are given to our Government to hold and protect forever. In presenting these instruments to the Library of Congress, it is my aim to give to the people of this country an opportunity to see and hear these rare Stradivari. They may be viewed at the Library of Congress by any one who wishes to do so. They may be heard in concerts held in the Library, and through the medium of the radio, by an even larger audience. If the appreciation and enjoyment of music in America will be advanced thereby, the purpose of my gift will have been fulfilled."

Table of Measurements

BETTS VIOLIN

Length	14 inches
Upper bouts	6 9/16
Middle bouts	4 7/16
Lower bouts	8 1/8
Upper sides	1 1/4
Lower sides	1 1/4
String length	12 3/4

WARD VIOLIN

Length	14
Upper bouts	6 1/2
Middle bouts	4 3/8
Lower bouts	8 1/16
Upper sides	1 1/8
Lower sides	1 3/16
String length	12 3/4

CASTELBARCO VIOLIN

Length	14 1/16
Upper bouts	6 5/8
Middle bouts	4 5/8
Lower bouts	7 3/4
Upper sides	1 3/16
Lower sides	1 3/16
String length	12 7/8

CASSAVETTI VIOLA

Length	16 1/4
Upper bouts	7 1/4
Middle bouts	5 1/8
Lower bouts	9 1/4
Upper sides	1 5/16
Lower sides	1 3/8
String length	14 3/8

CASTELBARCO VIOLONCELLO

Length	30 7/16
Upper bouts	14 1/16
Middle bouts	9 15/16
Lower bouts	17 7/8
Upper sides	4 9/16
Lower sides	4 9/16
String length	27 3/4

The Betts Violin (1704)

The outstanding instrument in the Collection is the famous " Betts " violin. Tradition has it that about 1830 this instrument was taken by its owner into the shop of the Messrs. Betts, the well known violin-makers in the old Royal Exchange in London, and was sold to them for 20 shillings, the owner believing that he was disposing of a brand new copy instead of a genuine Stradivari, in a perfect state of preservation. That there was some excuse for the owner's misunderstanding may be seen as the story progresses. For years Mr. Arthur Betts refused to sell this violin, although it is recorded that the bids for it ran up as high as 500 guineas, a very large price for a violin at that time.

Upon the death of Mr. Betts, the instrument passed on in his family, who held it for years, but eventually disposed of it to Mr. John Bone. He, in turn, in 1858, sold the violin to Mr. J. B. Vuillaume, the celebrated instrument-maker and dealer in Paris. Mr. Charles Wilmotte, of Antwerp, purchased the ' Betts ' from Vuillaume, and, after cherishing its possession for several years, disposed of it to Mr. C. G. Meier, who had long coveted it. Meier, in fact, looked upon the instrument with almost paternal affection, and was loath to allow any person to handle it. The next owner was Mr. George Hart, of London. When it came into Mr. Hart's possession, Charles Reade, the novelist, and a great lover of violins, wrote the following letter to the editor of the London *Globe*:

Sir, — As you have devoted a paragraph to this Violin, which it well deserves, permit me to add a fact which may be interesting to amateurs, and to Mr. George Hart, the last purchaser. M. Vuillaume, who could not speak English, was always assisted in his London purchases by the late John Lott, an excellent workman and a good judge of old Violins. The day after this particular purchase, Lott came to Vuillaume, by order, to open the Violin. He did so in the sitting room whilst Vuillaume was dressing. Lott's first words were, " Why, it has never been opened! " His next, " Here's the original bass-bar." Thereupon out went M. Vuillaume, half dressed, and the pair gloated over a rare sight, a Stradiuarius Violin, the interior of which was intact from the maker's hands. Mr. Lott described the bass-bar to me. It was very low and very short, and quite unequal to support the tension of the strings at our concert pitch, so that the true tone of this Violin can never have been heard in England before it fell into Vuillaume's hands. I have known this Violin forty years. It is wonderfully preserved. There is no wear on the belly except the chin-mark; in the centre of the back a very little, just enough to give light and shade. The corners appear long for the epoch, but only because they have not been shortened by friction, like other examples of the time. For the same reason, the edges seem high, but only because they have not been worn down. As far as the work goes, you may know from this instrument how a brand-new Stradiuarius Violin looked. Eight hundred guineas seems a long price for a dealer to give; but, after all, here is a Violin, a picture, and a miracle all in one; and big diamonds increase in number; but these spoils of time are limited for ever now, and, indeed, can only decrease by shipwreck, accident, and the tooth of time.

— I am, Your obedient servant, Charles Reade
19, *Albert-gate, May* 9, 1878

The extraordinary condition in which the "Betts" violin reached M. Vuillaume explains the belief of its earlier owner that it was a copy rather than an original.

Mr. George Hart sold the "Betts" to the Duc de Camposelice. From him it went to the Messrs. Hill, and they in turn sold it to Herr Jacques Zweifel, a German amateur. Some years later Hill bought the instrument back, acting on behalf of another client, Mr. R. E. Brandt, and later still Hill again repurchased the instrument and sold it to Mr. R. D. Waddell, of Glasgow. The Waddell Collection was purchased as a unit by the Rudolph Wurlitzer Company, of New York. Mr. Wurlitzer sold the violin to Mr. John T. Roberts, of Hartford, Conn., from whom it was purchased by Mrs. Whittall, together with the "Cassavetti" viola.

The "Betts" bears the date of 1704, which places it in the so-called "grand pattern" period, and it has long been acknowledged one of the most perfect and valuable violins in existence. The model is very full, being only slightly hollowed close to the purfling. The sound holes are beautiful, clear cut, graceful, and somewhat more upright than in other models. The scroll shows the bold outlines usually met with in Stradivari's work, and, as in most of the later models, the fluting is not quite so deep as in the earlier ones. The back is in two pieces, and the belly is of beautifully grained wood. The corners are unusually long, and the purfling extends as far as the space permits.

THE BETTS VIOLIN (front view)

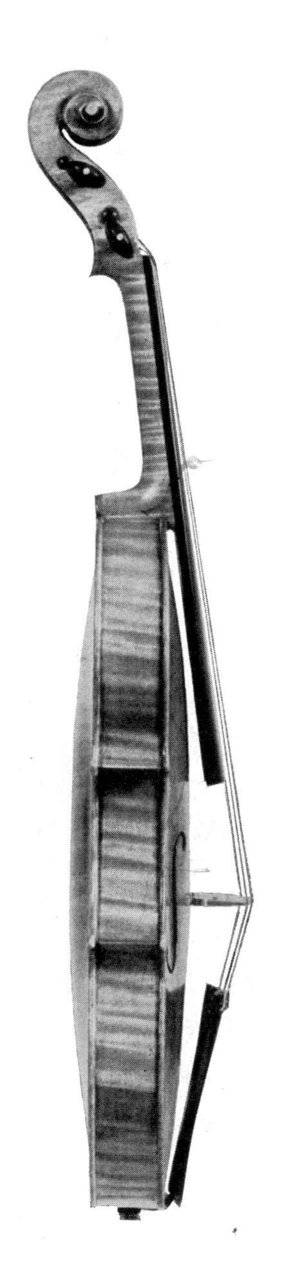

THE BETTS VIOLIN (side view)

THE BETTS VIOLIN (back view)

The Ward Violin (1700)

The "Ward" violin, dated 1700, has great beauty and perfection. The instrument takes its name from Mr. J. Ward, of London, its first recorded owner. This violin is quite different in arching and form from its companion violins, but with the "Betts" and the "Castelbarco" it forms a perfect trilogy.

Mr. Ward secured this violin from Mr. John Alvey Turner, a dealer in musical instruments, in 1860. It remained in his possession from that date until his death in 1907, when the Messrs. Hill purchased it from his estate. Herr von Donop was its next owner, and when he died the instrument passed into Switzerland, and from there to Mr. Arthur Beare; who, in turn disposed of it to Mr. Nathan Posner, of Brooklyn, from whom Mrs. Whittall purchased it.

The "Ward" violin still possesses its original neck as well as its original label. For modern usage, the length of the neck has been increased, but, to avoid using a new neck, wood has been skilfully grafted on to the original from the body of the violin to the peg box—just at the point where it joins the body. The back is in one piece, being marked by a broad curl which slants from left to right; and the sides are similar. The head is cut on the slab. The varnish, orange red, adds beauty through its soft texture.

THE WARD VIOLIN (front view)

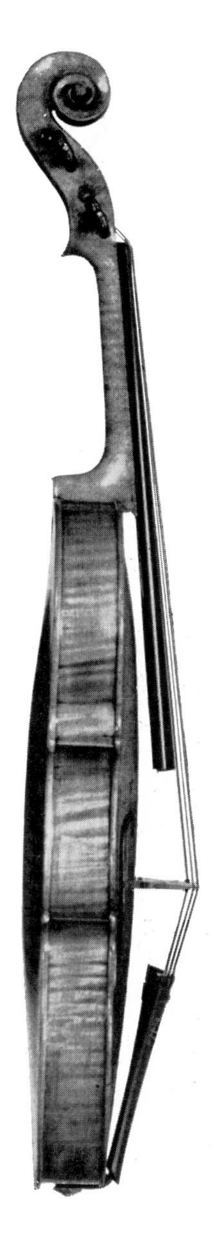

THE WARD VIOLIN (side view)

THE WARD VIOLIN (back view)

The Castelbarco Violin (1699)

Mr. Alfred Hill, in writing of the " Castelbarco " violin, says, " The violin is mentioned in our *Life of Stradivari* on page 48. When the book was written (in 1902) the figures on the label were 1701, an anachronism I long ago detected, for, although the label was genuine, the figures had been badly bungled, the correct date, in my opinion, being 1698 or '99; so, when the violin came into our possession I decided to right matters, and inscribed therein, once and for all, what I believe to be the original date, namely 1699. I always had a great admiration for this particular fiddle; it foreshadows the end of the period during which the ' long Stradivari ' was the instrument of the Master's predilection. Its beauty of workmanship and appearance are apparent to all, and its state of purity is beyond criticism."

This violin takes its name from a former owner, Count Cesare Castelbarco, of Milan, who was well known as an enthusiastic collector of instruments. In 1862 the Castelbarco Collection was offered for sale in London, where this violin was purchased by Vuillaume, of Paris. He disposed of it to Doctor Tesse, of Douai, but not long afterwards bought it back. Then it passed into the hands of Mr. David Laurie, who, in turn, sold it to the Messrs. Hill. In 1875 Mr. John Mountford purchased the violin, but some years later resold it to Hill, who again sold it to a Mrs. Renton. From her it came into the possession of Mr. Nathan Posner, of Brooklyn, from whom it was purchased by Mrs. Whittall.

The back of the " Castelbarco " is in one piece, the wood being cut on the slab and beautifully marked. On the sides the wood is cut on the quarter, but is of similar quality, while the belly is made of finely grained pine, opening out at the flanks. The varnish is golden orange.

THE CASTELBARCO VIOLIN (front view)

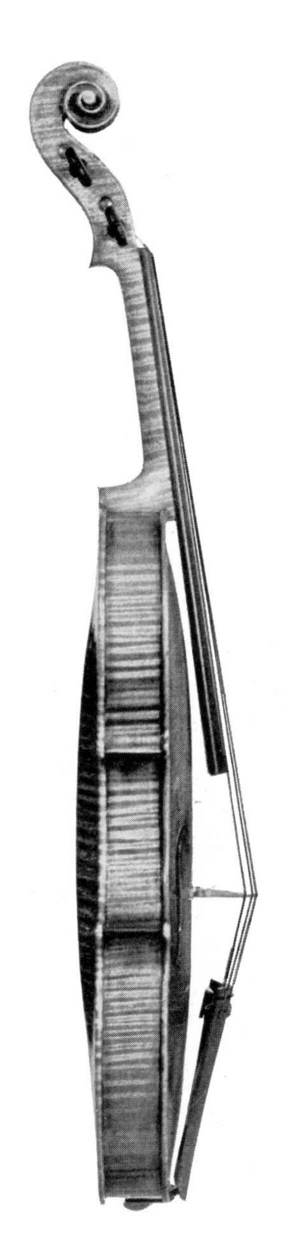

THE CASTELBARCO VIOLIN (side view)

THE CASTELBARCO VIOLIN (back view)

The Cassavetti Viola (1727)

Stradivari made this instrument in 1727, but the records showing its peregrinations are more meagre even than those of the violins. The earliest owner mentioned by name was M. Durand, a French amateur living in Paris, from whom the instrument was purchased to pass into the possession of M. Moulaz. At his death the viola was offered at auction in Paris, and was secured by Mr. David Laurie. Mr. Alexander Cassavetti, a member of a Greek family residing in England, then purchased the instrument, and it has carried his name since that time. In 1885 the viola is found in the possession of the Messrs. Hill, who disposed of it to Mr. Charles Oldham to complete his quartet of Stradivari instruments. Later the Messrs. Hill bought the viola back from Mr. Oldham and sold it to Baron Knoop. Again the Messrs. Hill repurchased the instrument, and then sold it to Mr. R. E. Brandt. In 1906 the "Cassavetti" was in the hands of an amateur living in Derbyshire, name unrecorded, from whom Mr. George Hart, of London, purchased it. In 1928 Mr. Hart sold it to Mr. Rodman Wanamaker, of Philadelphia. The viola was thus a part of the Wanamaker Collection when it was purchased as a unit by the Wurlitzer Company, of New York. They, in turn, sold the instrument to Mr. John T. Roberts, of Hartford, from whom Mrs. Whittall secured it.

The back of the "Cassavetti" consists of two pieces of beautiful wood marked by a small curl and cut on the slab. The wood used on the head and sides does not show the curl, but is also cut on the slab. The belly is made of pine of fine grain at the center, opening out on the flanks. The varnish is orange brown.

THE CASSAVETTI VIOLA (front view)

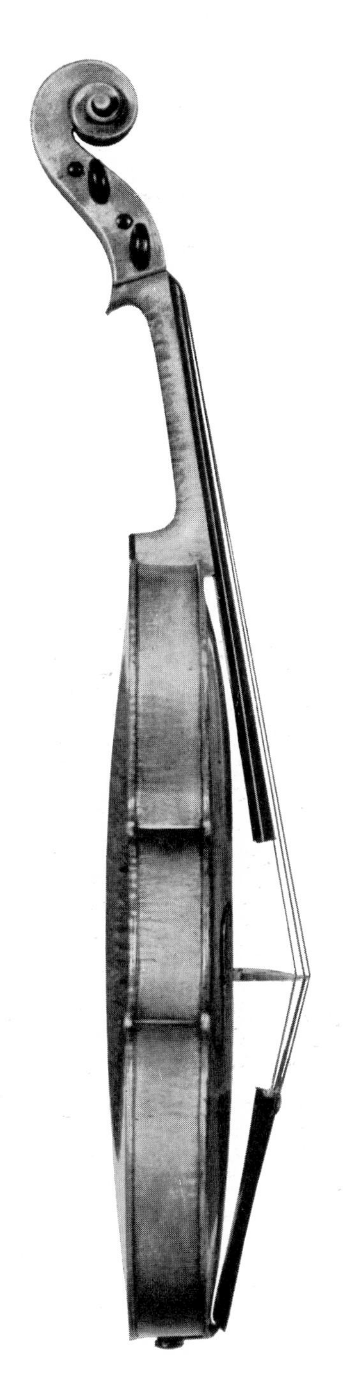

THE CASSAVETTI VIOLA (side view)

THE CASSAVETTI VIOLA (back view)

The Castelbarco Violoncello (1697)

This instrument, like the violin of the same name, formed a part of the celebrated Collection of Count Cesare Castelbarco, of Milan. It bears the Stradivari date of 1697, and was one of the three violoncellos of its period which have not been reduced in size. In speaking of this instrument, Mr. Arthur Hill says:

"I have always regarded it as a remarkable example of Stradivari's work, both on account of its beauty of form and its wonderful state of preservation. . . . I would furthermore add I know of no other existing Stradivari violoncello in such remarkably fine condition, for it is practically free from restoration. Its dimensions are as left by the maker, the cutting of the sound holes and the carving of the head, superb! and I repeat that, taken as a whole, it is amazing to think that the instrument should have preserved its present pristine state from the year 1697."

In 1862 the Castelbarco Collection was sold in London, and this violoncello was purchased by Vuillaume, of Paris, who sold it to Signor Egidio Fabbri, of Rome. From Fabbri the instrument passed into the hands of his son-in-law, the Marchese de Piccolellis. When the Marchese died, the violoncello was purchased by the Messrs. Hill, from whom Mrs. Whittall obtained it.

In making this instrument, Stradivari used poplar wood in the back, sides, and head, but pine in the belly. The varnish is orange brown.

THE CASTELBARCO VIOLONCELLO (front view)

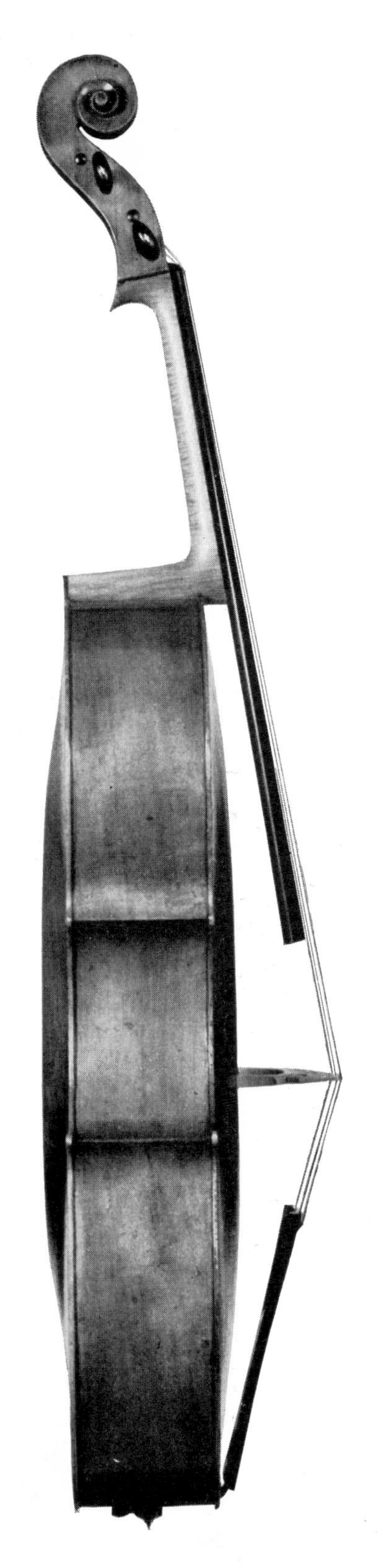

THE CASTELBARCO VIOLONCELLO (side view)

THE CASTELBARCO VIOLONCELLO (back view)

The Tourte Bows

Each of the five Stradivari instruments has a bow manufactured by the famous François Tourte, of Paris (1737–1835), who was at the height of his fame at the beginning of the 19th Century. Tourte stands alone in his position as the greatest bow-maker the world has known. "His father and elder brother were bow-makers also; and the reputation which attaches to the family name is not due to François alone — however, the latter has been called the Stradivari of the bow: and there is some truth in this, for, as Stradivari finally settled the model and fittings of the violin, so Tourte finally settled the model and fittings of the bow.

"An examination of Tourte's bows proves, that his first care was to select wood of fine but strong texture and perfectly straight grain, and his second to give it a permanent and regular bend.

"His indefatigable investigations led him to experiment in all kinds of wood which seemed likely to bring about the realization of his idea. He soon discovered that Pernambuco wood, found in Brazil, alone combined the requisite lightness and stiffness.

"Tourte never stamped his bows; however, they are sometimes found stamped with the name, but this is the work of another hand. His original nuts are usually of tortoise shell finely mounted in gold, but wanting the metallic slide on the stick, which was introduced by Lupot" (*From* Grove's "Dictionary of Music and Musicians.")

Two bows in the Collection — the "Baillot" and the "Russian" are among his most famous and most perfect productions. The "Baillot" at one time belonged to Mr. Julien Sauzay, who was a well-known violinist in Paris, being the direct descendant of M. Baillot to whom the bow formerly belonged, and from whom its name is taken.

In Cobbett's "Cyclopedic Survey of Chamber Music," Pierre Marie François De Sales Baillot (1771–1842) is described as a "French violinist and a supremely gifted quartet leader." Enlarging on this classification, the biographer adds: "Baillot was a man of the highest culture, originally destined for a bureaucratic career. As late as 1791 he accepted a position in the Paris Ministry of Finance, but continued practising the violin in his leisure hours. Considering that he was originally an amateur, his ardour for study must have been phenomenal, for he was in a position, a few years later, to secure a dual appointment as professor at the newly founded Paris Conservatoire, and solo violinist in the private chapel of the First Consul, Napoleon. In 1814 he set the seal upon his professional reputation by founding a series of quartet soirées, which stimulated the interest of musical Paris in the art of chamber music to a remarkable extent, and gave him a place in musical history as the most intellectual of the violinists of the French classical school."

The stick of the "Baillot" is round, made of dark-colored Brazil-wood of fine quality, mounted with tortoise shell and gold, with a tip of pearl. It is exactly as it was originally made. The stick of the "Russian" is also of Brazil-wood, but lighter-colored, with original mountings, the nut made of gold and tortoise shell, with mother-of-pearl eye surrounded by a gold ring; the tip is of mother-of-pearl mounted with gold. This bow was earlier the property of a Russian violinist who secured it from Emile Germain, of Paris.

L'Envoi

Now in a thought, now in a shadowed word,
Now in a voice that thrills eternity,
Ever there comes an onward phrase to me
Of some transcendent music I have heard;
No piteous thing by soft hands dulcimered,
No trumpet crash of blood-sick victory,
But a glad strain of some vast harmony
That no brief mortal touch has ever stirred.

There is no music in the world like this,
No character wherewith to set it down,
No kind of instrument to make it sing.
No kind of instrument? Ah, yes, there is;
And after time and place are overthrown,
God's touch will keep its one chord quivering.

Edwin Arlington Robinson

From "Children of the Night," Richard C. Badger & Co. Copyright, 1927